MW01063317

Risk Management in Plain English: A Guide for Executives

Enabling Success through Intelligent and Informed Risk-Taking

Norman Marks, CPA, CRMA

First Edition

Contents

Introduction

In 2015, I published *World-Class Risk Management*. I am pleased that it has been very well received and influenced many risk practitioners.

But, the management of risk remains poorly understood (in my opinion) and even more poorly practiced.

In 2017, COSO[1] published a needed update to its 2004 *Enterprise Risk Management – Integrated Framework.* Renamed *Enterprise Risk Management – Integrating with Strategy and Performance*, it is an improvement but leading risk practitioners and thought leaders (including me) find it less than satisfactory. We do not believe it will move the needle on risk management in the right direction far enough.

In 2018, we expect an update to the other principal document guiding risk management. ISO[2]'s global risk management standard, 31000:2009, will be replaced by 31000:2018. However, this too has shortcomings and is not expected to make a significant difference.

The biggest gap is in understanding that risk management is not about avoiding harms. It is about increasing the likelihood of success.

It is about understanding what might happen and acting to increase the extent and likelihood of success.

My 2015 book addresses that, but is directed primarily at practitioners.

---

[1] The *Committee of Sponsoring Organizations of the Treadway Commission*, www.coso.org

[2] The *International Organization for Standardization*

This book focuses more on principles and on helping those in leadership positions understand how risk management can help them succeed.

It is deliberately shorter and written at a higher level so it can be consumed by executives and board members as well as by practitioners.

I am open to comments at nmarks2@yahoo.com.

Norman Marks, 2018

I.   Executive Summary

Why do most executives and board members see little operational value in risk management?

According to surveys, they consider it as something required for compliance and not how they direct and run the organization to achieve its goals. It does not help them set and then execute their strategies.

They do it more to satisfy third parties (such as regulators and investors) than because they believe that it helps them succeed.

They consider it as a separate activity rather than integral to running the operation.

"Only 13% of [C-level] respondents believe their risk management processes support, at a high level, the ability to develop and execute business strategies"

Deloitte: *Exploring Strategic Risk*

That is because traditional risk management is about managing a list of so-called risks, bad things that might happen. Just look at all the studies and reports about "emerging risks" and the demands from the regulators to disclose the risks that might adversely affect the organization and its results.

But, risk management is really about increasing the likelihood of **achieving your objectives**.

It is not just about avoiding harm.

It is about:

- *Anticipating* what might happen
- *Assessing* whether that would be OK
- *Acting* as needed
- *All so you can increase the likelihood and extent of success*

In *World-Class Risk Management*[3], I said:

> "The effective management of risk enables more informed decision-making, from the setting or modification of strategy to the decisions made every day across the extended enterprise."

When you make intelligent and informed decisions, you increase the likelihood of success!

Managing risk is neither new nor separate from running the business

Executives have been managing risk all their lives! Perhaps I should say they have been *taking* risk every day – but not without regard for the consequences.

When they have a decision to make, which happens every day, they:

- Make sure they understand the problem
- Consider what might happen if they took no action and whether that would be acceptable
- Review their options
- For each, consider what might happen
- Pick the best option (recognizing that one option is not taking any action) after weighing all the potential consequences
- Act, monitor, and adjust as needed

When I say that "they consider what might happen" and "weigh all the potential consequences", I am not saying that they only think about the things that could go wrong.

They consider *all* the potential consequence, both the positive and negative, before making their decision.

---

[3] Published in 2015 and available on *Amazon*

We talk about "weighing the pros and the cons", the "pluses and minuses".

We say that "on balance" we prefer one option over another.

We say that we have *decided to take the risk*. Maybe we take the risk after putting other measures in place. But we are still taking risk; we are not always trying to 'manage risk' as so many risk professionals and consultants say.

We take risk because it is in our best interests. The benefits outweigh the potential cost and other negatives.

We make an intelligent (we hope) and informed decision.

That is risk management.

Let me repeat that:

> **Risk management helps you make informed and intelligent decisions.**

We have an objective.

But how do we get there? How do we achieve or exceed it?

Many things can happen as we strive to reach our objective.

Some of those are good and some not so good.

We want to take advantage, where possible, of the good and avoid the more serious harmful events and situations.

We cannot predict with certainty[4] what will happen.

But.....

The more we are able to anticipate what might happen, the better we can be prepared and the better we will be able to respond.

---

[4] This is where the concept of 'uncertainty' comes in. Some define 'risk' as the effect of uncertainty on objectives – but that language is not plain English and is not spoken in this book.

Informed decisions are far more likely to be the right decisions.

This is not new for executives. They have been making decisions that weigh the pros and cons their entire career.

But, are they doing it in a *disciplined and systematic fashion*?

Are they relying on information that is reliable, current, complete, and accurate?

Have all potentially affected parties been involved and have they contributed to the discussion?

Is it only the top executives that are taking risks?

No.

Risks are being taken pretty much every minute of every day, at all levels of the organization.

A decision by a middle manager can have disastrous effects on even the largest enterprise.

Consider the *Deepwater Horizon* disaster. Without argument, it was a disaster of massive proportions for BP and its CEO.

But who made the decisions that contributed to the explosion on the oil rig?

The decisions were not made by the CEO or any of his direct reports.

A report by the *Joint Investigation Team of the Bureau of Ocean Energy Management, Regulation and Enforcement* (BOEMRE) and the U.S. Coast Guard pointed to:

- A defective cap installed by BP's contractor, Halliburton

- Decisions by BP managers about the installation process, and

- The failure of BP and partner Transocean employees to say anything when early indications of a problem appeared.

While the CEO is ultimately responsible for the actions of every employee, he or she does not make every decision that can have a significant effect on objectives.

In fact, the CEO and his direct reports may not (arguably, cannot) be aware of all the decisions that are being made, all the significant risks that are being taken.

If risk management is about:

- *Anticipating* what might happen
- *Assessing* whether that would be OK
- *Acting* if needed

... how can a CEO and his team, let alone the board, know with any level of confidence that people are doing this well?

How can they know people are making the decisions they would like them to make, and taking the right level of the right risks?

Effective risk management requires processes to provide leadership with the assurance they need, the peace of mind, that all significant decisions are intelligent and informed.

> If people are making intelligent, informed decisions and taking the desired level of the right risks, then there is a much higher likelihood of achieving the enterprise objectives and strategies.

There cannot be any certainty around achieving objectives because:

- There will always be surprises – luck, if you prefer
- Even the best efforts at anticipating what might happen can be wrong

But investing in increasing the likelihood of getting it right can pay off in spades!

Risk management is NOT about managing a list of risks – whether you call that list a risk register or risk profile. That is a useful exercise, which we will discuss later, but not the heart of risk management.

It's about:

- Setting the right objectives
- Selecting the best strategies for achieving them
- Running the operation day-to-day and making the right decisions to achieve your objectives
- Doing the above intelligently, with the help of the right people and based on the best available information (given time and other constraints)

In other words….

It's all about effective management.

Here's a hypothetical story to explain what I am saying.

The executive team has come to the point in their monthly meeting where they review the report of the Chief Risk Officer.

The CEO invites the CRO to join them.

> CRO: "Here is my monthly risk report. As you can see, every risk, whether strategic, operational, technology, or other, remains within our defined risk appetite. While the level of a few individual risk areas has increased, they have not escalated to merit a 'high' risk rating. We are continuing to monitor them."

> CEO: "Thank you. Do any of you have any comments or questions?"

CIO: "Yes, I do. I see that you are reporting that cyber risk has increased, although it remains at a yellow rating, which I believe indicates that it needs to be monitored but no additional actions are required. Can you tell me why you see the risk level increasing?"

CRO: "Certainly. The Chief Information Officer's assessment is that opening our new office in Poland increases the risk level. It's not only that we now have additional network points that may be vulnerable, but as I understand it crime groups from the region may choose us as a target."

CIO: "Thank you. The CISO had discussed that with me and we had come to that same conclusion. But you also show IT systems risk as increasing. Is that because we are adapting our systems so they can support additional languages such as Polish and currencies such as the zloty?"

CRO: "That is correct. I think that is what you and I agreed last week."

CIO: "It is."

He is interrupted just as he was about to ask another question.

COO: "You show supply chain risk as increasing. I agree with that assessment. Is it because there may be disruption in our supply of products to the new market in Poland?"

CRO: "That is correct. The VP of Supply and Logistics is concerned about transportation during winter as well as the possibility of rail strikes."

EVP Sales: "You know, I am also concerned about Poland. You show revenue-related risks, including credit risk, as within tolerance. But I only see the likelihood of hitting our first year targets for Poland as 85%. I don't that's as OK as your report indicates."

CRO: "But when we met, you said that the overall risk to revenue was not high and the CFO said the same about credit risk."

CEO: "Am I missing something here? It sounds like your risk report tells us about enterprise-level risk in a number of categories, but doesn't help us with specific programs and projects. Is that right?

CRO: "Well I am following the global risk framework and what our consultants told us when we set the program up. This is their recommended report format, with a heat map on the second page. I would be happy to give you a separate report on Poland-related risks."

The CEO is clearly disturbed and asks the CRO to step out. He then continues.

CEO: "Clearly the Poland project is increasing our risk in a number of areas. Do we need to have the CRO run a separate report or should we talk about it now, without him?"

COO: "Poland is my project. I would like everybody involved to stay after the meeting. Let's talk about whether the prospects for Poland justify taking these risks. If we are going to potentially miss our revenue targets and, at the same time, increase risks around credit, cyber, and so on, perhaps we should reconsider."

CEO: "Good idea. But I want to be part of this discussion as we have made this a key part of our strategy, with Poland being just the first step into Eastern Europe, in our discussions with the analysts and investors. In fact, it is possible that after considering what we now know we may want to delay or move into Croatia first. Let's finish the rest of the agenda and then continue. Can everybody stay a little longer?"

The meeting continues without the CRO.

My point: it's not about managing risks, even at the enterprise level.

It's about managing the organization to deliver success: making informed decisions.

II.   Are we taking too much or too little risk?

The traditional approach to risk management is about whether the organization is taking too much risk – the kind that can lead to losses.

This is the concern of the regulators. They believe that investors want to know "how risky" the company is.

The regulators are concerned, rightly or not, about the possibility of loss – even to the extent of failure of the organization.

They are much less concerned about whether the organization is achieving its potential – and that requires not only not taking too much risk but also taking risk when the opportunity justifies it.

When you are running the business, you have to do both: avoid unnecessary loss and seize opportunities for gain.

A simple example is when you go to the casino.

- You may place a limit on your losses by deciding how much you can afford to lose and stopping when you get there. Of course that takes discipline.

- But you can avoid any losses either by not going to the casino or by limiting yourself to the restaurant, showrooms, and your hotel room.

- You gamble because of the reward. Perhaps it's because you believe (usually in error) that you have an edge and are more likely to win than lose. But, more often it's because it's a pleasurable activity.

The same applies in business.

- Being in business is a risk.

- You can place a limit on the amount you can lose (for example, by establishing a limited liability company, purchasing insurance, or otherwise keeping the potential for loss within your established limits).

- But you are taking the risk, the potential for loss, because there is (you believe) a greater likelihood of gain than there is of loss.

No responsible executive would run the business by only paying attention to the potential for loss.

Every organization, whether public, private, governmental, etc. needs to take risk to thrive.

But you want to take the right amount of the right risks.

You take risks through informed and intelligent decisions.

You have to decide whether taking the risk is "worth it".

For example, imagine you are at the casino and have the dice in your hands. Would you bet $100 if there was an even chance of losing the $100 and winning $100? You probably would not, unless you place a value on the thrill.

But would you bet the $100 if the odds are 2:1 (in your favor) of winning $100 vs. losing $100? You probably would – assuming that the loss of $100 would not be calamitous (for example, if you absolutely needed it to get home or if it were your spouse's money).

You certainly would throw the dice if you could afford to lose and the odds are clearly in your favor.

When I say that risk management is about making informed decisions, I mean that you understand (with a reasonable level of uncertainty) the odds and size of the winning and losing bets.

"Can I afford to throw the dice?" is the first question. The second is "are the odds in my favor or not" (to an acceptable degree – a slight edge may not be enough)?

Let's consider the second first. We will look at the first in chapter IX, Risk Appetite.

Good and bad can flow from a single event, situation, decision, or throw of the dice.

Focusing only on the downside is silly.

You need to know all the possibilities if you want to make an informed decision.

The possibility for gain as well as loss

There are many sources of risk[5] and it doesn't make sense to consider only potential negative effects. Consider these potential adverse events or situations and comparable positive events or situations:

A downturn in the economy affects your customers and results in your failing to achieve revenue and earnings targets.	An uptick in the economy affects your customers and results in achieving higher than expected revenue and earnings.
A customer experiences financial problems and fails to pay you monies owed on time. Your revenue and earnings targets are affected, as well as cash flow. If it is a significant customer, the cash flow disruption might affect your ability to fund projects and lead to further deterioration of future	A customer lands a major new contract and substantially increases its orders of your products. Your revenue and earnings targets are positively affected, as well as cash flow. You are able to fund or accelerate projects that lead to further improvements in future earnings.

---

[5] A source of risk is *where* something can happen that might affect the achievement of one or more objectives

earnings.	
A breach of your information security leads to the theft and publication of your customers' personal information, including credit card information.	A breach of your competitors' information security leads to their loss of customers who come to you with their orders.
The failure of one or more employees to comply with regulations is made public and results in an investigation and fine by the regulators – a compliance failure that may be disruptive to the business and affect both revenue and cost.	You maintain a first-class reputation for safety, environmental protection, and so on that gives you an edge over your competitors.
The loss of one or more key employees leads to delays in key initiatives or loss of customer relationships, in turn leading to a failure to achieve revenue and earnings targets.	You are able to hire and retain employees who bring new ideas and improvements to existing products and services that to higher revenue and earnings results.
The vendor of materials critical to your manufacturing process suffers an event that disrupts his and therefore your business. As a result, customer satisfaction and revenue are adversely affected.	The vendor of materials critical to your manufacturing process introduces a new generation product that, when included in your products and services, allows you to excite your customers. As a result, customer satisfaction and revenue are positively affected.

A major project experiences difficulties and delays. Possible adverse effects include loss of cash flow, increased costs, delays of a product launch that customers are clamoring for or in the implementation of a computer system needed by the organization to drive improvements in efficiency or customer satisfaction. All of these might affect earnings, customer satisfaction, market share, and other enterprise objectives.	There is a breakthrough in a major project and it is completed under budget and early. Possible effects include improved cash flow, reduced costs, an early product launch that customers are clamoring for or the early implementation of a computer system needed by the organization to drive improvements in efficiency or customer satisfaction. All of these might affect earnings, customer satisfaction, market share, and other enterprise objectives.

Traditional risk management only considers the first column.

The effective manager considers all possibilities, both columns.

The level of risk is not a single point

Not to complicate things, but there is generally a *range* of potential effects, each of which has a different likelihood of occurring.

For example, if you have an account in an overseas bank, the value of that account in your native currency is likely to fluctuate. It might increase and it might drop in value. The extent of the variation could be large or small.

The chart below shows the likelihoods of different levels of gain or loss on a hypothetical overseas account as currency rates fluctuate.

Experts in assessing risk of this type use models that take into account both the possibility of loss and that of gain.

Decision-makers should take into account the range of possibilities rather than, as traditional risk managers might suggest, believing that risk can be represented by a single point.

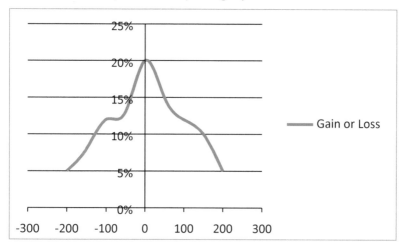

The traditional approach to risk management only thinks about the possibility of adverse effects.

But the intelligent executive is always looking at all the things that might happen and how they might affect the business.

The smart risk practitioner knows how to help management calculate the likelihood and extent of loss.

The *very* smart risk practitioner helps the managers calculate both the likelihood and extent of loss *and* the likelihood and extent of gain.

III. Risk and the CEO

It's trite to say that the CEO is the chief risk officer.

But, in a sense, that is correct.

The CEO is responsible for the management of the entire organization, which includes how decisions are made and risks are taken.

He (or she)[6] needs to know that:

- When people come to him for a decision, they have thought everything through:
    - the current situation and why there is a problem
    - the alternatives
    - what might happen under each scenario
    - why their recommended option is best
- When people make decisions that don't need his involvement, they have similarly thought everything through

He needs to know that the right risks are being taken.

He needs to know that the processes surrounding decision-making, in other words around risk-taking, are reliable.

He needs to know that people are *thinking before acting*.

He also needs to know that when surprises happen, not only is he informed but appropriate actions are taken.

How does that happen?

It starts with the CEO himself: how he makes decisions and the example he sets for others.

---

[6] I will generally use the pronoun 'he' but obviously all positions can be held by males or females.

It's how he behaves, makes decisions, and sets expectations for decision-making.

Asking the right question

For example, great questions he might ask (of others and of himself) include:

> "How confident are you in these projections, estimates, and assumptions?"

> "How likely are we to hit these numbers?"

> "Why do you say that you are 85% confident?"

> "How can we improve the likelihood of success?"

> "What can we do to minimize the downside?"

> "Why do you believe the upside potential justifies taking the risk?

> "Have you involved everybody whose functions or objectives might be affected by this decision?"

> "What alternatives have you considered? Why did you pick this one?"

> "What if….?"

> "How will you keep track of what happens later and how will you know how and when to respond?"

It comes down to making sure that every decision by the CEO is only made after thought has been given to all the potential consequences of that decision.

Smart questions that provide assurance that the individuals bringing a proposal to the CEO have 'thought it through' are essential to smart decision-making.

Here's a hypothetical story about what happened when a CFO (Jerry) presented his forecast for the next quarter to the executive team:

> CFO: "We project beating the budget and the earnings forecast we gave the analysts by 2% in the next quarter. Revenue is expected to increase by 5%, outpacing the increase in expenses."
>
> CEO: "How confident are you in these numbers?"
>
> CFO: "Pretty confident. My team worked closely with the Sales and Marketing staff and others to put the numbers together. Of course, we are dependent on closing a couple of major deals in the quarter. Tom [the Sales and Marketing VP] told me he fully expects them to close."
>
> CEO: "What does 'pretty confident' mean? Are you 95% confident or is it more like 85%?"
>
> The CFO turns to Tom.
>
> CFO: "Tom, would you agree with 90%?"
>
> Tom: "I guess so. A lot could still go wrong but I am sure we can work through any problems."
>
> CEO: "What problems?"
>
> Tom: "Well, we will need our new generation product to be released on time and the Legal department is looking at some new state regulations. But Mark [the head of Engineering] says the new product is almost ready and Mary [the general counsel] thinks the new regulations are unlikely to affect us."
>
> CEO: "How likely are any of these, or anything else for that matter, to cause us to fall short of Jerry's numbers?"
>
> Tom: "Well, I guess that there's a 10%-15% chance. But there's also a decent chance, perhaps 5%, that our customers will order more and we would then beat Jerry's forecast."
>
> The CEO looks around the room.

CEO: "Has anybody got anything else to share? Anything else you are managing that could affect, either positively or negatively, our results for the next quarter?"

The Senior Vice President for Supply and Logistics, Lisa, reluctantly joins the conversation.

Lisa: "There is a possibility of a supply chain disruption. A few days ago, our air freight carrier send me an email saying that there might be an airport strike next month. He said there was a 10% chance of one and that would clearly impact sales. Tom and I have a meeting planned for tomorrow to talk about this and how we can be prepared."

CEO: "OK, Jerry, it looks like there is a good chance that we won't hit your numbers. Can you meet with everybody and get back to me with answers to these questions?

1. How likely are we to at least meet our earnings forecast?
2. How likely are we to encounter problems that could cause us to miss it?
3. What is being done about each of them and is it enough?
4. What can we do to improve revenue and earnings, perhaps building a bit of a cushion in case one of these situations occurs?

I want answers in the next couple of days and we will put this on the agenda for our executive team meeting next week. I also want to hear ideas on how we can report our forecast going forward so it reflects what might happen and what we need to do about it."

In sophisticated organizations, proposals presented to the CEO might include required discussions of what might happen, both good and bad, for each option.

For example, 'what if' sections might explain the likelihood and magnitude of different consequences, including:

- The effect on cash flow

- Projected margins, recognizing that there is almost always a *range* of possible outcomes

- How cyber risk might be affected

- Compliance implications

- How the organization's reputation might be affected

- The level of confidence in the processes and controls relied on to assure success

Cognitive bias

One danger for the CEO (indeed, for every human) is what is called 'cognitive bias'.

This is an area that every executive and key decision-maker should study and seek to understand as it can lead to mistakes that can have a significant effect on the whole organization. There are multiple studies and guides, but here are some simple examples:

- A bias against an individual coming to you with information such that you instinctively greet their data with disbelief and discard it – and the opposite, always trusting the views and information of those you like

- A tendency to see things the way you want them to be, instead of the way they are

- Trusting your memory or your 'gut' rather than objective data

- Believing that you have seen the situation before and what worked last time will work this time, when perhaps some of the facts are different

Leading by example

The CEO sets an example.

When the CEO makes decisions without asking for information or input from his team, or fails to consider alternative strategies and their consequences in a systematic fashion, a policy that requires others to make informed decisions is less likely to be followed.

Policies and standards, such as a risk management policy, can sit on the shelf unless leadership leads by example.

Policies and standards only work if they reflect how the business *should* be run, not only to avoid failure but to achieve success.

Just as the CEO wants his executives and others across the organization to keep their eyes on the goal, to work towards success, so should policies and standards.

The CEO wants his team to weigh all the potential consequences, both good and bad, before making an informed and thoughtful decision.

Policies, standards, and procedures need to reinforce and support that forward-looking stance.

The CEO should insist that every individual charged with enabling and supporting the management of risk (the Chief Risk Officer, or CRO, for example) has a forward-looking, *business* perspective.

The CEO and the CRO

Every CRO should see their job as helping the organization and the management team <u>succeed</u>, not just avoid failure.

The CEO should take responsibility for the mind-set and ability of the CRO to enhance decision-making.

The CRO should not be the chief "risk hunter," always looking for what might go wrong.

The CRO should be the evangelist for smart decisions, making sure that:

- Everybody knows that when it comes to decisions, they are expected to be thoughtful, gather all relevant and useful information, involve others who have input or who might be affected, and then do what is right for the organization as a whole.

- The processes for obtaining reliable information, analyzing what might happen, and doing what is right are sound, up-to-date, and practical.

- When needed, cross-functional discussions are facilitated to allow the constructive and open discussion of where we are, what might happen in the future, and what to do about it.

- Actionable information about what might happen, including the likelihood of achieving objectives, is communicated to all those who need it – from the board to team leaders.

The CEO should obtain assurance from his team, including the CRO, that:

- Decisions are thoughtful.

- Everybody understands what the organization is trying to achieve, its objectives, and how their actions contribute to success or failure.

- People have the information they need to make informed decisions.

- Intelligent mistakes are forgiven, reckless success is not.

- Information about what might happen (adverse risks and positive opportunities) is not only obtained but communicated.

- Bad news is communicated as rapidly and honestly as good news.

Nothing is free.

Processes and systems that enable effective risk management, effective decision-making, require an investment in people, technology, and time.

An investment in decision-making, which is an investment in risk management, is worth its weight in gold…. as long as it is focused on success management, not doom management.

The CEO should be an example and mentor in effective management, including decision-making – which is the heart and soul of risk management.

IV. Risk and the Executive Leadership Team

Each individual executive (and the CEO as an individual) is responsible for making intelligent and informed decisions, setting an example for others, and demanding thoughtful and considered decisions from their teams.

But as a team, the executives have what might be called a *governance* role.

While the board may be responsible for governance at a high and principled level, the executive team runs the organization day-to-day. They set the expectations for the management of risk by every decision-maker, in other words the informed and intelligent taking of risk.

Responsibilities include:

- Ensuring that everybody is working together for shared goals – achieving the objectives of the enterprise as a whole. That includes not only every operational manager and executive but the CRO and his team.

- Ensuring that everybody not only knows what the enterprise objectives are, but understands what is expected of them if those objectives are to be achieved. It is not sufficient to "link" personal objectives to enterprise objectives (the practice at some organizations). Achieving enterprise objectives relies on the actions and decisions of individuals and those individuals need to know what those are.

- Making sure that individuals and teams put achieving enterprise objectives ahead of their personal or team objectives.

- Working effectively as a team, sharing information and resources as needed. Coming together to make the many decisions that involve or affect two or more executives.

- Providing oversight of decision-making and risk-taking processes, procedures, systems, and policies.

- Understanding the 'big picture', the aggregate effect of everybody's individual efforts.

- o Monitoring performance against enterprise objectives, which includes not only knowing where we are now (Key Performance Indicators and Metrics, or KPI) but what might positively or adversely affect us going forward (Key Risk Indicators, or KRI). This is an enhancement of traditional performance reporting to integrate 'risk'.

- o Acting as necessary to change course, modify decisions and so on, to increase the extent and likelihood of success.

- o Where it is possible that events of situations might arise that would significantly affect the organization (positively and negatively, and perhaps affecting more than a single enterprise objective), monitoring them and acting as needed. This is what many organizations call risk reporting, but traditional risk reporting is not linked to objectives and only considers the downside.

- Modifying practices, policies, strategies, and so on as needed. Constantly asking whether everything is working as well as it should.

Managing risk is managing what might happen – and the executive team should ensure that every decision it makes and every decision its people make are as informed as possible and made after appropriate consideration and thought.

On a periodic basis (and in some dynamic environments this may be as often as monthly or even weekly), the executive leadership team should review a list of the more significant 'risks' facing the organization. This is a list of risks that tend to be continuing rather than those that are handled in day-to-day operations and decision-making.

Most often, this is a list of potential harms, but world-class organizations should also pay attention to potential opportunities.

The periodic review of this list of risks is covered in chapter VI.

Working to the same objectives

In each of the companies I worked for, the executive team and the board established enterprise objectives.

However, in none of them was an adequate job done to make sure that everybody was working towards these as shared goals.

Individual and team objectives were set by the individual and his or her manager.

In some cases (not all), the related enterprise objective was identified.

What is needed is for the owner of an objective to identify what is needed from others.

They, in turn, should have objectives to provide what is needed.

This cascades as necessary throughout the organization.

This is not an easy task, but it needs to be addressed in every organization if they hope to have everybody working towards shared goals – in practice, not just in theory.

V.   Risk and the Executive

The executive will live or die by the quality of his or her decisions.

It is in his best interests to be able to make quality decisions that:

- Incorporate a reliable assessment of the current situation and what is likely to happen if no action is taken

- Consider whether that is desirable, not only for himself and his team but for the organization as a whole

- Are based on reliable, current, complete and accurate information – not only from information systems but from individuals and teams, including interested parties outside the organization (such as service providers, agents, vendors, partners, and so on)

- Understand the options available

- Are made after assessing the pros and cons of each option in a systematic and disciplined fashion then weighing all the potential consequences together

- Result in taking the risks that not only are right for the organization but are in line with the desires of top management and the board

- Are then monitored so that adjustments can be made if things start to turn out differently

Making decisions is hard – if you want to consistently make good ones.

We seem to spend our days 'fighting fires' and feel a need to make decisions quickly.

Some decisions can be made quickly.

But some need time.

The effective executive knows the difference and is willing to think before acting.

There are a lot of tools that will help an executive, or any decision-maker for that matter, understand and then analyze what might happen.

- Models

- Monte Carlo simulations

- Game theory

- Brainstorming and other workshops

- And so on

Different problems will require the use of different tools.

For example, decisions by a financial institution on whether to purchase or sell financial instruments often benefit from the use of sophisticated models.

However, decisions by a manufacturing company on when a new product is ready to be launched will more frequently benefit from a cross-functional discussion with every involved department contributing.

Executives typically have a span of control that includes multiple departments or units.

It is essential that the executive see the bigger picture, understanding how his teams are performing overall.

For example, a sales executive may own the enterprise objective of achieving $xx in revenue at a gross margin of yy%.

Each of his five direct reports is responsible for a piece of that.

The executive needs to know how they are doing overall, what decisions they are making, and whether those are the decisions he wants them to make.

When are they sacrificing margin to close a large deal? When are they holding firm?

Do they have sufficient guidance from him as to when it is possible to make a deal outside the optimal parameters – for example, because of a deal's longer-term potential?

The sales executive should also know how his people's actions might affect goals and objectives owned by others.

For example, there may be objectives relating to cash flow and credit. (If not enterprise objectives, these are likely to be subordinate objectives, required to achieve enterprise objectives such as Earnings per Share.)

There will be times when consultations are required with other departments. If the executive is not himself involved, then he needs to know that they still happen and the right decisions are made for the company as a whole.

This is all standard management practice. But it is also managing risk.

The executive and the CRO

The executive will make good use of the CRO and his team.

For example, the CRO might provide a facilitator for cross-functional decisions. He might provide tools and methods for assessing what might happen.

At SAP, when there is a major potential deal[7], the sales team is required by policy to bring in a facilitator from the risk office. The risk officer will chair a meeting with all potentially affected parties, such as finance, legal, sales, credit, and operations. They will consider the pros and cons of the potential deal and whether, on balance, it should be pursued. Perhaps changes are required to the terms before the contract would be acceptable. The key is that the risk officer is making sure everybody's concerns are considered and the best decision made for the company. Additional meetings may be scheduled to follow up on progress if the risk justifies them.

The CRO's team may also pull together reports from different parts of the organization to help the executive see the bigger picture.

---

[7] This is based on practices when I worked with SAP.

The extended enterprise

There are some 'risks' that relate to activities *outside* the organization[8]. For example:

- Changes in laws or regulations, including changes as a result of court decisions, regulatory interpretations of existing laws or regulations, and so on

- Actions by competitors, such as pricing, the introduction of new products, marketing campaigns, the opening of new stores, and so on

- Changes in the expectations of the community. For example, a greater emphasis on 'responsible' sourcing, avoiding conflict minerals, and so on

- Legal actions against the organization; sometimes, legal actions against a competitor or similar organization can indicate a change in risk

- Actions by partners, vendors, and such. For example, the introduction of new products by a major vendor, or the loss of a relationship with a channel partner

Executives need to know about such changes.

They need to know how they may affect the organization and the achievement of its objectives.

They need to know that the organization is prepared for such changes and able to make intelligent and informed decisions in response.

One area that frequently does not get sufficient attention is the fact that many *business decisions* are made by people outside the company.

The majority of organizations rely on service providers, channel partners, agents, and so on ("partners"). Individuals within those

---

[8] In the ISO 31000:2009 global risk management standard, these are described as changes in the external context.

organizations can make decisions that not only affect the partner but also our company.

For example, a partner may:

- Decide to use children in its labor force
- Decide not to invest in safety training for individuals who work at your location
- Fail to perform critical internal controls and security mechanisms that put your operations and information at risk
- Sell your products to organizations or nations in violation of sanctions
- Put relationships with its other customers ahead of yours

Executives need to understand how the actions and decisions of others, especially those relied on to perform critical services, might affect the success of the organization.

Some companies send partners in the extended enterprise questionnaires that address known areas of concern. But the understanding obtained from such questionnaires is limited.

The key is to:

- Understand how the organization and its objectives may be affected
- Assess whether the level of risk is acceptable
- Assess whether the organization is prepared should an adverse event occur (such as the service provider failing)
- Take actions as necessary, which may include selecting different partners or adopting different strategies

Cross-functional decision-making

Very often, executives need to work together to solve a problem and make the right decision.

One of the best examples of risk management was a decision made by the Vice President, Procurement in Singapore for a global technology company I worked for. This is how I described it in *World-Class Risk Management*.

> The vice president responsible for procurement needed to decide how the company was going to source a number of vital materials. He had received bids from about a dozen vendors, each of which had different prices, payment terms, manufacturing capacity, and performance history (including their history of on-time delivery, product quality, customer service, and so on). He had the option of selecting a single vendor (which would enable him to optimize his cost) or a number of vendors (allocating his purchases among them and spreading the risk that one might fail in some way).

> This smart executive didn't make the decision by himself. He made it in collaboration with the senior vice president of manufacturing, the vice president of quality, the region's vice president of finance, and others.

Multiple objectives and risks to them were involved in this single decision:

- Margin and earnings per share objectives would be affected (positively or negatively) by the price paid for critical materials

- Revenue and earnings per share objectives would be affected if the quality of products was less than expected by customers. They might return products and require replacement; require costly repairs; switch to other vendors; and so on. Even if poor quality manufacturing was detected before the products were shipped, rework is expensive as are inspection and related costs. Shipment of the product to customers might be delayed, again affecting revenue and EPS targets

- Reputation objectives might be affected if it became known that the company shipped less than high quality products

- Objectives relating to the company's share price would be affected if the company missed any of the above targets

What is important is that the Vice President, Procurement recognized that not only his personal and team objectives would be affected by the vendor decision, but those of his peers and of the enterprise as a whole would be as well.

The decision had to balance all the potential outcomes, both positive (reduced price, for example) and negative.

Again, that is what risk management is about:

- *Anticipating* what might happen

- *Assessing* whether that would be OK

- *Acting* as needed

- *All so you can increase the likelihood and extent of success*

All of this is so you can be successful, achieving objectives.

It's the art of management, frankly, as much as it is the management of risk!

VI. Risk Reporting, Review, and Appetite

The heart of risk-taking is decision-making.

But there is more to the management of risk.

On a regular basis, we need to know:

- Are we on track to achieve our objectives?
- If there is a possibility of falling short, are the appropriate actions being taken and are they likely they will succeed?
- If there is a possibility of exceeding our objectives, are we doing enough to seize those opportunities?
- Where there are significant threats, especially those that might affect the achievement of multiple objectives, are we doing enough?
- Do we have a good handle on what might happen going forward? Are we looking in all the right places, using all the resources we should, analyzing the possibilities reasonably accurately, and using that information to make intelligent and informed decisions?
- Are we working well together, with reliable and timely information, to make those decisions necessary for success?
- Are we in fact, taking the right risks?

The key question is whether, considering all the things that might happen (the likelihood of each and how that would affect the objective), we are going to achieve each of our objectives.

Some progress was made by Dr. Robert Kaplan when he added risk indicators to his concept of a balanced scorecard.

However, it is not enough to know whether the risk indicators are high, medium, or low. Successful managers need to know the likelihood of achieving each objective.

One of the problems with traditional risk management is that it considers risks singly.

But, a single objective might be affected by multiple risks.

For example, let's say the objective is to open a new office in a new region and deliver $10m in new revenue. The success or failure of the initiative might be affected by one or more of these:

- Delays in the readiness of the office to open
- Delays in the hiring of key personnel
- Problems with the systems that will be used to support the new office
- Cuts in competitors' prices for similar products or services
- Changes in the economy and the demand for your products or services
- New regulations that will affect the ability to provide products and services at a price that delivers the desired revenue and profits
- Issues in the supply chain
- And so on

It is possible that no single potential issue is sufficient to derail the program. But, the executive team needs to consider the full range of risks.

The simplistic approach is to take each one and multiply its likelihood and potential impact (as noted elsewhere, there is a range of potential effects and likelihoods for each effect). Then they are added together to get the total risk.

But that is neither real life nor mathematically correct. The likelihood of two separate incidents occurring is the *product* of their individual likelihoods.

The correct mathematical approach should be to consider which combinations of risks would be sufficient to derail the program. Then, probability theories can be used to assess their likelihood.

A recommended risk report

I developed a report format that might be helpful.

For each objective it shows where we stand to date and the likelihood of achieving our objective (within a reasonable range). It goes further, indicating the likelihood of falling short and the likelihood of exceeding the objective. Further information, such as the details of the things that might cause us to fall short and the degree by which we will miss the target, can be linked to each cell in the report.

An example is shown on below.

Objective	YTD Status	Fall short	Achieve target	Exceed target
Revenue growth of 10%	9.85%	15%	80%	5%
EPS improvement of 5%	8.00%	10%	80%	10%
Maintain customer satisfaction levels	98.00%	8%	90%	2%
Improve market share by 5%	5.00%	20%	70%	10%
Introduce new product on time and budget	72.00%	30%	65%	5%

A report like this provides useful, actionable information.

The executive responsible for each target, as well as the executive team and the board, can ask questions that will lead to actions that increase the likelihood and extent of success.

The concept of "risk appetite" has been popularized by consultants, regulators, and others. It is defined[9] as:

> The types and amount of risk, on a broad level, an organization is willing to accept in pursuit of value.

This is not particularly useful.

It's not about managing risk; it's about managing the achievement of objectives. In order to achieve objectives, you want risks to their achievement to be within desired levels. (The topic of risk appetite is discussed more fully in chapter IX.)

What is more useful is determining the acceptable level of risk to the achievement of objectives. That is less an "amount of risk" and more the *likelihood* of failing to achieve the objective *by a specified amount*. For example, your risk appetite is not $500,000 when your goal is to achieve $10,000,000 in revenue growth; instead, you are willing to accept a 5% likelihood of missing the target by $500,000.

But, your willingness to take risk is always affected by the potential for reward and is more nuanced than a single amount or level of risk.

For example, if your target for revenue growth is 8.5%, would you be willing to accept:

- A 90% likelihood of getting to 8.5%, but a 10% possibility of only achieving 8.0% growth and zero chance of exceeding the target?

- An 80% likelihood of attaining 8.5%, with only a 5% possibility of falling short at 8.0% and a 15% likelihood of getting to 9.0%? In other words, would you be willing to take a 5% risk of falling short if there was a 15% chance of beating the target?

In the table above, I colored each of the metrics accordingly (green is acceptable but red is not).

---

[9] COSO's *Enterprise Risk Management Framework: Integrating with Strategy and Performance* (2017)

A list of risks or a heat map

Many organizations provide executives and the board with a list of risks. They indicate which are high, medium, or low based on some measure (typically reflected in the likelihood of a quantified loss).

But while that looks good, it is difficult to assess how each of the listed risks might affect the strategies and objectives of the enterprise.

An alternative to a list (whose use is encouraged in the COSO 2017 ERM Framework) is a heat map, such as shown below.

Heat Map

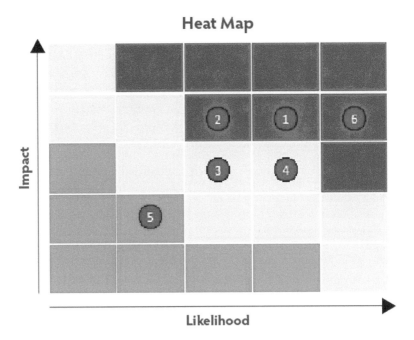

The axes may have values (for impact) and percentages (for likelihood), or simply described as going from low to high.

The colors are intended to reflect whether each of the risks (1-6) are high, medium, or low. High is supposed to indicate that the level of risk is unacceptable, green is acceptable, and the others need to be watched and possibly treated as well.

But how does this help the leaders of an organization?

The leaders on the board and in top management may be *concerned* about risks, but they are *focused* on achieving objectives and delivering value to their stakeholders.

The heat map does not tell them how these risks might affect what they are trying to achieve. Without the connection, managing risk is seen as somewhat incidental to performance and to achieving objectives.

Reviewing a list of risks

Nevertheless, the periodic review of a list of the more significant risks is a useful exercise, especially when it highlights issues that might affect *multiple* objectives and may continue for some number of months.

For example, the risk of a cyber breach can affect objectives relating to:

- Revenue. For example, it can lead to: the loss of intellectual property that jeopardizes market leadership; the disclosure of customers' confidential information and the loss of those customers; an inability to bill customers; or damage to the company's reputation such that both current and future demand is adversely affected.
- Cost and earnings. For example, there may costs to contain and then repair any damage; penalties and fines from regulators; or the need to acquire additional products and services top reinforce the company's defenses.
- Major projects, such as the completion of a major systems implementation or the rollout of a new product or service.

Assessing a risk that affects multiple objectives is a little more complex.

But the key question remains whether the risk is one the organization should accept.

If not:

- What action should and will be taken and will it be completed within an acceptable timeframe?
- Will it bring the risk within acceptable limits?
- Who is responsible for taking the necessary actions?
- Who is making sure it all happens?
- Who is monitoring to ensure we will know if the level of risk changes (for example, as the result of actions by a competitor)?

A list can also help those responsible for disclosing the organization's top risks in filings with the regulators (such as the annual and quarterly filings in the USA with the Securities and Exchange Commission).

But it doesn't really help you drive performance.

It also only highlights the risks that might derail your initiatives, not the opportunities you might seize to optimize results.

The risk du jour

There is a trend today to put a lot of attention on the 'risk du jour', the risk that captures the headlines. Examples include:

- Cyber
- Reputation risk
- Third party risk
- And so on...

But reality interferes with the ability to totally eliminate such risks.

The only way to eliminate these risks is to close down the business.

If you want sophisticated information systems, or to introduce products and services that rely on connectivity with customers, you have to take a certain level of cyber risk.

If you want to do business in perhaps the majority of foreign nations, especially if you have to engage a partner, you have to accept a certain level of reputation risk as well as third party risk.

As usual, it's all about whether the risk-taking is informed and intelligent – and that has to be based on the potential effect on the business as a whole.

In other words, it's not about cyber or reputation risk. It's about how a cyber breach or damage to your reputation will affect the business and the achievement of its objectives.

Unfortunately, many of the experts in each of these areas (cyber, reputation risk, third party risk, and so on) fail to help the executive team and the board understand how they might affect the success of the organization as a whole.

If the risk is not expressed and understood in terms of its *potential effect on the business*, how can either the board or senior management know how much to invest in addressing the risk when there are alternative uses of the funds, such as new products, marketing strategies, and acquisitions?

To illustrate, here is an excerpt from *World-Class Risk Management*:

> In my first year as vice president of internal audit at a technology company, the head of security and the IT executive responsible for information security asked for a meeting. They said that they needed my support to persuade the senior executives that they needed to encrypt the hard drives on their laptops. They explained the obvious: the senior executives' laptops held critical customer, financial, and operating information including the company's strategies and plans, as well as financial forecasts, product cost information, and more. At that time, the technology to encrypt hard drives was not inexpensive and it would make the executives' use of the applications on those devices more difficult. I could see why the management team was balking at the idea, both from a cost and an ease-of-use perspective, when the benefit was only

to limit the potential damage should their device be lost or stolen – even though that happened with disturbing regularity!

I asked the two managers if they had done a risk assessment. They said they had. I was more than a little doubtful and asked whether they had assessed all the risks relating to technology within the business. They said that not only had they completed a full IT risk assessment, but that the potential for somebody with technical acumen to obtain a lost or stolen laptop, and use the confidential information it retained, was the top risk.

When they said this, I asked if their risk assessment had considered the fact that the organization's diverse global operations used multiple financial systems (they had everything ever invented), which were cobbled together with Excel spreadsheets for financial reporting and to consolidate operating information. Didn't they think that was a significant business risk? I also asked whether they believed the company's network was secure, given that they had yet to implement any intrusion detection or prevention systems.

In short, they had not stepped back and thought about whether the risk they had identified was significant to the business as a whole and its overall objectives. It looked important, sounded important, but was only a minor issue.

While a list of risks is interesting, knowing whether you are likely to deliver performance and achieve objectives is the path to success.

Each executive team, working with the board, should establish how it wants to measure performance and receive reports on risk. It is useful if both receive reports in a similar style.

But the emphasis should always be on optimizing performance and not on managing risks out of context.

How effective is your risk management program?

There is another report that both the board and the executive team should receive, on at least an annual basis.

That is a report that provides assurance that the processes for all of the above, the management of performance and risk, the taking of risks through informed decisions, are in good shape – adequate, if you like that term.

Management is responsible for all of these processes. Management should therefore take responsibility for them being up to the task.

Management means the CEO.

The board should hear whether the CEO believes that the program is effective, helping people understand what might happen and make informed and intelligent decisions.

He or she may delegate that to another executive, such as the CFO or the Chief Risk Officer.

But the CEO should make him or herself comfortable with the assessment, as it is the core of effective management of the whole organization.

There are several ways to perform such an assessment, which are discussed in detail in *World-Class Risk Management*.

One way is to consider whether a set of principles for effective risk management has been achieved. Both the COSO ERM Framework (2017) and the ISO 31000 global risk management standard suggest a number of principles. My recommended principles are based on the ISO 31000 standard (2009 version, whose principles are superior to those in either the 2018 update or the COSO set):

1. Risk management enables management to make intelligent decisions when setting strategy, planning, making decisions, and in the daily management of the organization. It provides reasonable assurance that performance will be optimized, objectives achieved, and desired levels of value delivered to stakeholders.

2. Risk management provides decision-makers with reliable, current, timely, and actionable information about the uncertainty that might affect the achievement of objectives.

3. Risk management is dynamic, iterative and responsive to change.

4. Risk management is systematic and structured.

5. Risk management is tailored to the needs of the organization and updated/upgraded as needed. This takes into account the culture of the organization, including how decisions are made, and the need to monitor the program itself and continually improve it.

6. Risk management takes human factors (that may present the possibility of failures to properly identify, analyze, evaluate or treat risks) into consideration and provides reasonable assurance they are overcome.

Another way is to answer the question:

> Do I have reasonable assurance that the processes for managing risks and the likelihood of achieving objectives meet the needs of the organization, enabling informed decisions and driving success?

The internal audit team should also provide an assessment of risk management. That is required both by their professional standards[10] and by several national corporate governance codes.

The question above is a useful basis for the internal audit assessment, as is asking about the achievement of the principles above or in the ISO 31000 global risk management standard. While COSO's ERM Framework also has principles, I do not believe them to be as useful a basis for assessing the management of risk. (More on this topic can be found in *World-Class Risk Management*.)

---

[10] *The International Standards for the Professional Practice of Internal Auditing*, from the Institute of Internal Auditors.

VII. Risk Management and the Board

Most of the guidance on risk management, whether from consultants or risk management associations, focuses on the board reviewing a list of risks.

As noted above, it may be interesting to review a list of risks.

But the board should be focused on performance.

Risks have to be taken if the organization is to succeed.

The question is whether risk-taking is wise and prudent, and that should be judged based on enterprise objectives rather than on a discussion of risk without context.

Is risk management effective?

How does the board obtain assurance that the right level of the right risks is being taken?

It's not by debating with management whether they have the right list with the right assessments.

It's by requiring and then debating the CEO's assessment of how well risks are being taken – how well decisions are being made, because that is where, in practice, risks are taken or not.

As noted above, one useful method for assessing the effectiveness of risk management is to determine whether a set of principles (I suggested six) have been achieved.

The board should obtain the CEO's assessment first, not that of the CFO or chief risk officer. Hold the CEO accountable. If he or she refers the question to another executive, then ask whether he agrees with and supports that assessment.

It is certainly important to obtain a formal report from the internal audit function that related processes and controls provide reasonable assurance that the right risks are being taken.

But, don't rely exclusively on their work. The board should insist on the CEO sharing his or her assessment.

When the board takes risk

There are some risks that the board, itself, is taking.

For example, the members are responsible for:

- CEO succession planning
- The performance of the board and its committees in providing corporate governance as well as supporting the executive team with their insight and expertise
- Executive compensation

Issues related to any of the above could affect the success of the organization.

The board has to assess that risk and decide what to do about it.

For example, do they take actions to increase executive compensation to retain or attract top talent, or are they concerned how that might be perceived by investors and regulators?

Are they satisfied with their own performance or should they replace some of their members with others expert in fields like risk management, information technology, or China?

It is important that the board recognizes that it is taking risk itself and needs to be confident that it is the right level of risk.

Some believe that the board should have at least one member that is a recognized expert in risk management.

That may be appropriate for financial services and other sectors where complex assessments of risk (such as assessment of financial portfolio risk) are common.

But in my experience using common sense and asking the right questions will enable the board to be comfortable in its oversight of risk management.

Risk and the board's agenda

On a regular basis, the board should review two reports:

- A report that shows performance for each of the agreed performance objectives. It should not only show progress to date, but indicate the likelihood of achieving the objective – as discussed earlier

- A report that shows those risks that management believes are significant enough to adversely affect the organization's success. The board may ask that certain risks of interest to them be included. These are typically longer-lasting risks (i.e., they won't include risks that are addressed routinely by operations) and may affect multiple objectives. In addition, these may constitute the risks that are disclosed in filings with the regulators

Discussion of risks should not be separate from discussions of performance – as they are two elements of the same conversation. It is only by discussing risks to each objective that the board can assess whether the management team is likely to deliver on its targets.

The Hudson Bay Company integrated its discussions of strategy and risk. In other words, it did not have separate board discussions of performance against strategy and of risk.

The board will not only want to know that management has good processes for taking risks (i.e., making decisions) but is taking appropriate actions on the more significant risks to the organization's success.

The board should not take on the responsibility for identifying, assessing, or addressing risk (with a few exceptions, as noted earlier).

That remains the responsibility of the management team.

Instead, the board should obtain assurance that management is not only capable but is in practice disciplined in its decision-making processes – as those are where risks are being taken.

The independent CRO

A growing number of organizations have appointed a chief risk officer (CRO). The next chapter discusses his or her role, but many regulators and consultants are pressing for the CRO to report directly to the board and to be independent of the management team.

That can cause serious problems.

For example, the management team may decide that the CRO is responsible for risk management and not them. If more risk is taken than desired by the board, then that is the fault of the CRO and his team.

Too often, management feels that the risk office is a drag on performance, preventing them from taking risk essential to achieving objectives approved by the board.

If not actively an obstacle, the risk office is seen as a bureaucratic operation that slows down management's ability to run the organization.

Similarly, risk officers may see operating management as 'cowboys' and their job is to 'rein them in'.

In other words, they neither trust each other nor work effectively together.

That is not the path to success.

They need to work together.

There has to be a mutual understanding that:

- Operating management not only 'owns' risk but is responsible for:
    - Identifying it
    - Assessing it
    - Evaluating whether risk should be taken or not
    - Acting as necessary to modify the risk
    - Ensuring that senior management and the board receive the information about both performance and risk they need
    - Working effectively with the risk office
- The CRO and his team are responsible for:
    - Helping operating management and the organization as a whole succeed
    - Helping management understand and then take the right level of the right risks
    - Ensuring that all decision-makers have the processes, systems, guidance, and information they need to know what risks to take
    - Working with management to ensure senior management and the board receive the information they need

The board should ensure that the CRO and management work effectively together. The downside is too great if they do not.

There is a big BUT!

The risk officer should be able to escalate a situation where one or more members of management are taking a level of risk that is beyond what the board or top management has approved.

The risk officer should be able to do that without inappropriate obstruction or punishment by management.

So, while the risk officer and staff should see their job as helping management take the right level of risk, making informed decisions, they should also have access to senior management and, if necessary and appropriate, the board.

VIII. Risk Management and the Risk Office

As explained above, positioning the CRO and his team as the sheriff, and tasking him or her with watching to make sure that the cowboys in operating management don't cross the line and take too much risk, is itself a serious source of risk.

No, the risk office should be there to *help* management make informed and intelligent decisions, which result in them taking the risks necessary to achieve objectives: the desired level of the desired risks.

It may be necessary, to comply with regulations, for the CRO to report to the board. But, the board should ensure that the CRO is working as a partner to management and not assuming the role of a watchdog.

Management needs to continue to own the responsibilities for taking risk and reporting to top management and the board. They may be assisted by the risk office.

In many organizations, the CRO is responsible for maintaining the lists of risks[11] and using it as the basis for reports to top management and the board.

But the risk assessments should be owned, not by the CRO, but by management.

If the CRO disagrees with management's assessment of risk, that should be escalated to executive management and, if necessary, to the board. However, the CRO should seek to reach agreement as a partner to management, not to confront management as the corporate police.

The CRO can help with:

- Ensuring there is a common language for risk management. People not only use the same language but have a shared understanding of what it means

---

[11] These lists may be referred to as risk registers, risk inventories, or risk profiles.

- Consolidated reporting on behalf of management to the executive team and the board

- Facilitating risk discussions, especially across multiple parts of the organization

- Maintaining risk policies, owning risk management systems, and otherwise facilitating the management of risk

- Working with the board and top management to define risk appetite (where useful), what will be disclosed in regulatory findings, and bringing significant issues to their attention should operating management not do so first

- Monitoring risk management policies and processes and working with management to upgrade them as the need arises

- Assisting management when there are acquisitions, helping them integrate those operations from a risk management perspective

- Mentoring existing and training new management and staff in the organization's expectations, policies, procedures, and systems for managing risk

- Providing other support as needed

More details on how risk management should function in an organization are discussed in *World-Class Risk Management*.

IX.   Risk Appetite

Earlier, I said:

> The concept of "risk appetite" has been popularized by consultants, regulators, and others. It is defined as:
>
>> The types and amount of risk, on a broad level, an organization is willing to accept in pursuit of value.
>
> This is not particularly useful.
>
> It's not about managing risk; it's about managing the achievement of objectives.

While this is true, the regulators like and sometimes require that an organization define and disclose (to a degree) its risk appetite.

There are times when a risk appetite and reports of whether it is being exceeded are useful.

As I said earlier, when making a decision that exposes you to a loss (such as when you are considering making a bet), it is essential to know if you can afford that loss.

Risk appetite statements are supposed to guide decision-makers, telling them how much the organization is willing to put 'at risk'.

- Limits on risk-taking are set and approved by top management and the board. More than one limit is generally required as there are multiple sources of risk and it usually doesn't make sense to try to aggregate them. For example, how do you aggregate safety and credit risks?
- Decision-makers are to stay within those limits.
- Monitoring is in place to ensure the limits are not exceeded.
- On a periodic basis, compliance with the limits is reported to top management and the board.

But the amount of loss you are willing to expose yourself to will vary depending on the potential for gain or value. So the COSO definition, which is used broadly by regulators, is not particularly useful.

The term doesn't really make sense when you are talking about compliance or safety risk. No reputable organization will say anything other than they have no tolerance for any compliance violation or safety incident. But the only way to eliminate these risks is to exit the business.

In real life, there is a limit to the resources an organization is willing to commit to avoiding compliance or safety problems.

The concept is most useful when we are talking about a financial portfolio, such as those held by banks, insurance companies, and other financial institutions.

These are excerpts from Deutsche Bank's description of their 'risk appetite and capacity' in their Annual Report 2016:

> Risk appetite expresses the aggregate level of risk that we are willing to assume within our risk capacity in order to achieve our business objectives, as defined by a set of minimum quantitative metrics and qualitative statements. Risk capacity is defined as the maximum level of risk we can assume before breaching regulatory constraints and our obligations to stakeholders.

> The Management Board reviews and approves our risk appetite and capacity on an annual basis, or more frequently in the event of unexpected changes to the risk environment, with the aim of ensuring that they are consistent with our Group's strategy, business and regulatory environment and stakeholders' requirements.

> In order to determine our risk appetite and capacity, we set different group level triggers and thresholds on a forward looking basis and define the escalation requirements for further action. We assign risk metrics that are sensitive to

the material risks to which we are exposed and which are able to function as key indicators of financial health.

Reports relating to our risk profile as compared to our risk appetite and strategy and our monitoring thereof are presented regularly up to the Management Board. In the event that our desired risk appetite is breached under either normal or stressed scenarios, a predefined escalation governance matrix is applied so these breaches are highlighted to the respective committees. Amendments to the risk appetite and capacity must be approved by the Group Risk Committee or the full Management Board, depending on their significance.

The Reserve Bank of Australia published its *Risk Appetite Statement* in 2017. It said (excerpts):

The Bank faces a broad range of risks reflecting its responsibilities as a central bank. These risks include those resulting from its responsibilities in the areas of monetary, financial stability and payments system policy, as well as its day-to-day operational activities.

The risks arising from the Bank's policy responsibilities can be significant. These risks are managed through detailed processes that emphasise the importance of integrity, intelligent inquiry, maintaining high quality staff, and public accountability.

The Bank is also exposed to some significant financial risks, largely due to it holding Australia's foreign exchange reserves. It accepts that the balance sheet risks are large, and manages these risks carefully, but not at the expense of its policy responsibilities.

In terms of operational issues, the Bank has a low appetite for risk. The Bank makes resources available to control operational risks to acceptable levels. The Bank recognises that it is not possible or necessarily desirable to eliminate some of the risks inherent in its activities. Acceptance of some risk is often necessary to foster innovation and efficiencies within business practices.

....

The Bank aspires to be among the world's leading central banks, measured by the quality and effectiveness of its operations. This requires ongoing development and innovation in its operations through strategic initiatives which often carry significant risk. The Bank has a low appetite for threats to the effective and efficient delivery of these initiatives. It recognises that the actual or perceived inability to deliver strategic initiatives could have a significant impact on its ability to achieve its objectives as well as its reputation.

The Bank's Executive meets regularly to discuss the major initiatives. A framework is in place to ensure that these initiatives are prioritised appropriately, and that the associated risks are well managed and reported on a consistent basis.

....

The Bank holds domestic and foreign currency-denominated financial instruments to support its operations in financial markets in pursuit of its policy objectives. These instruments account for the majority of the Bank's assets and expose the balance sheet to a number of financial risks, of which the largest is exchange rate risk. The Bank does not aim to eliminate this risk as this would significantly impair its ability to achieve its policy objectives. Instead, the risks are managed to an acceptable level through a framework of controls. The Bank acknowledges that there will be circumstances where the risks carried on its balance sheet will have a material impact on its financial accounts. The Bank regards it as desirable to hold sufficient reserves to absorb potential losses.

The Bank has a very low appetite for credit risk. The Bank manages this risk carefully by applying a strict set of criteria to investments, confining its dealings to institutions of high creditworthiness and ensuring that exposures to counterparties are appropriately secured, wherever feasible.

....

Information Technology (IT) risks cover both daily operations and ongoing enhancements to the Bank's IT systems. These include:

> **Technology Service Availability – Prolonged outage of a core RBA system:** The Bank has a very low appetite for risks to the availability of systems which support its critical business functions, including those which relate to inter-bank settlements, banking operations and financial markets operations. Service availability requirements have been identified and agreed with each business area.
>
> **Security – Cyber-attack on RBA systems or networks:** The Bank has a very low appetite for damage to Bank assets from threats arising from malicious attacks. To address this risk, the Bank aims for strong internal processes and the development of robust technology controls.
>
> **Technology Change Management:** The implementation of new technologies creates new opportunities, but also new risks. The Bank has a low appetite for IT system-related incidents which are generated by poor change management practices.

Describing your risk appetite as "low" sounds good but has no practical meaning.

What is "low" and how would you know whether your actual level of risk is "low"?

How would you know whether you are taking more risk than advisable?

In practice, organizations need to set and describe their risk appetite in meaningful terms.

The risk appetite statement has to guide decision-makers, helping them understand whether they are taking more risk than they can afford to take.

I believe most financial institutions establish quantitative "triggers and thresholds" (Deutsche Bank), have methodologies for calculating the level of risk, and compare that level of risk to their risk appetite for their portfolios.

But some prefer to talk about "a strict set of criteria[12]" (Australian Reserve Bank).

In practice, smart executives make investment decisions based on a careful weighing of the potential for both gains and losses, with a minimum expected return – but within limits.

The most practical way of setting limits is through traditional spending limits, where authorization from more senior individuals (up to the full board) is required as the size of the investment required increases.

The concept is that if you can delegate the authority to spend, you can delegate the authority to take risk.

But how do you set limits?

---

[12] While the COSO *ERM Framework* relies on risk appetite, the ISO 31000 risk management standard prefers the term risk criteria.

The traditional method is set a limit in dollar terms, a method that considers the potential loss that might be incurred and the likelihood of that loss. In other words, risk – P * I.

That might make sense when you are talking about things that might happen that have a clear quantifiable effect – such as the possibility of a customer failing to pay monies owed or the loss of value of an investment.

But:

- As noted earlier, there is usually a *range* of possible effects and likelihoods. This can be calculated (the area under the curve formed by the range) but unfortunately too many simplify by picking one point in the range.
- The consequences of some potential events or situations are less readily quantified. For example, few if any would put a dollar value on the loss of life, non-compliance with regulations, and so on.

Nevertheless:

- The board and top management should determine which areas of risk they want to monitor against limits.
- They should establish metrics that provide useful and actionable information about whether people are taking the desired level of the right risks.
- They should ensure, if at all possible, that decision-makers can be guided to stay within those limits.

In practice, the last of these three bullets is hard to achieve. The relevance of an enterprise objective and risk limit may be difficult for a middle manager to understand and apply in decision-making.

For example, there may be many credit managers in an organization. Each is responsible for working within a business unit and granting (or declining) credit to a range of customers. How can any of them know whether the limits established for total credit risk are going to be exceeded by one of their decisions? How can any of them know that there is substantial room within the credit limit to allow a deviation from strict policy and grant credit that enables a highly profitable deal?

Another, more complex but realistic story, involves three people: the executives responsible for Human Resources (Jerry), IT (Joy), and Operations (Melody).

- Jerry has a decision to make. He has an open position for a recruitment officer after losing an experienced individual. He is concerned with achieving his primary objectives, on which most of his bonus is based, of staying within budget and retaining or hiring competent personnel within his department. Jerry has short-listed two candidates. The first is a junior member of his department with great potential but little experience and fewer contacts. The second is an experienced recruiter who is currently working for a competitor. But the second not only will command a salary that will stretch Jerry's budget but he would have to pay a fee to a personnel agency. One option Jerry is considering is delaying the hiring for a couple of months and then hiring the experienced candidate. That way, he can say he has maintained quality in his department and stayed within budget.

- Melody is responsible for operations at the company's manufacturing locations around the world. Her bonus is based, in large part, on the timely rollout of a new product. The project will drive a significant portion of the revenue growth that is the company's top objective for the year. It appears to be on track, but it depends on completion of updates to the manufacturing system. Joy informs her in their monthly meeting that she expects to be able to complete the system changes on time.

- But Joy needs to fill at least one position in her system testing team before the changes can be tested and finalized. Normally, it is fairly easy to hire the staff she needs. It usually takes less than six weeks. The work that the new staff member would have to complete should only take two weeks and the target date for completion is three months away.

- Only if everybody comes together (probably literally coming together in a meeting) to understand how the actions of one can affect another, and set aside personal goals in favor of achieving enterprise goals, will Jerry make the right decision.

What is called the 'inter-relationship of risks' (when the actions of one person affect others, whose reactions affect yet others, and so on) is an issue that needs attention from the management team. The CRO can help as he or she can (hopefully) see the bigger picture.

It's a problem for which there is no one-size-fits-all solution.

But, if each performance objective owner can identify what is needed from whom, and then they (in turn) can determine what they need from others, and so on, the problem may be addressed.

The key is that everybody's compensation is driven by what is needed from and by them to achieve enterprise objectives.

Only when you understand how your actions affect the achievement of enterprise objectives can you understand the consequences of those actions. Only then can you know, hopefully with guidance from the senior management team, how the risk to enterprise objectives you are taking is acceptable.

X. Converting Risk Management into Action

How do pull all of this together?

How does the CEO, the executive team, and the board make sure there is 'effective risk management', which I translate (in plain English) as making sure that decision-makers understand what might happen as they lead, direct, and manage the organization, then make appropriate and informed decisions?

I believe it starts, as does this book, from the top.

The CEO sets an example by ensuring that not only do his decisions consider all the things that might happen, both good and bad, but that all proposals brought to him cover the possibilities as well.

The CEO also sets the expectation that his direct reports, separately and as part of the executive management team, will similarly make considered decisions.

In turn, every executive sets the appropriate example and expects their staff to do the same.

In this way, there is an emphasis on intelligent and informed decision-making.

Each executive has to consider whether they are getting all the information they need to make informed decisions. The information must be:

- Complete
- Accurate (within an acceptable tolerance)
- Current
- Timely
- In a consumable and actionable form

Unfortunately, surveys show problems with the quality and reliability of information.

For example, most managers reportedly rely on their instincts rather than seeking all available information – and, again according to surveys – the vast majority are not even aware of all the information that is available.

A few years ago, I was leading a discussion with a group of CFOs at the Harvard Club in New York. I asked them how quickly they could obtain a current cash position if the CEO called them right then and asked for information about available cash for an acquisition. The answers varied from a week to a month!

Many organizations still have information systems that do not provide, on demand, the information managers need to make quality decisions.

In this era of dynamic change, it is essential that decisions be made relatively fast (but not in haste) and that requires an improvement in the capabilities of many organizations.

The COSO ERM Framework update of 2017 makes the suggestion that when a strategy, program, or project is initiated the things that might happen to affect its success (i.e., risks) are identified. While these risks might easily change over time, the concept is sound. The risks are then monitored so that changes can be made to the strategy or execution over time.

The CEO, executive team, and the board need to receive <u>periodic reports that show not only the current level of performance but also the prospects of success for each enterprise objective</u>.

Discussing the reports, and what needs to be done to improve the extent and likelihood of success, should be a priority at every executive committee and board meeting.

On a periodic basis, which should be as frequent as needed given the nature of the business and its risks, it is useful to <u>'take stock' of the continuing risks</u> that might affect the success of the organization.

Often, these are things that might happen that would affect multiple objectives.

The traditional risk reporting is limited to a list of the things that might go wrong. However, such a report could easily (and with value) include the potential for positive events and situations.

Some call these 'strategic risks'. But all risks that need to be managed have a potential effect on enterprise strategies – so it is not a term I embrace.

It is better, always (in my opinion) to <u>use plain English</u> rather than make everything more complex by using technical terms that increase the likelihood of a misunderstanding.

After all, managing what might happen is a part of regular and effective management. It should not need a separate language – with a few exceptions, such as when calculating risk related to a financial portfolio.

If we keep to plain English and require all discussions and explanations in plain English, everybody can understand and contribute.

If something cannot be explained in plain English, then there's a problem either with the communicator or with what he is trying to say.

The management of risk may need specialized staff and systems to support it. That is something that every organization needs to consider – there is no one-size-fits-all answer, just as there is no one-size-fits-all ideal risk management computer system.

As I said in chapter V, risk management is about:

-   *Anticipating* what might happen
-   *Assessing* whether that would be OK

- *Acting* as needed

- *All so you can increase the likelihood and extent of success*

All of this is so you can be successful, achieving objectives.

It's the art of management, frankly, as much as it is the management of risk!

About the Author

Norman Marks, CPA, CRMA is a semi-retired chief audit executive and chief risk officer. He is a globally-recognized thought leader in the professions of risk management and internal auditing and remains an evangelist for "better run business", focusing on corporate governance, risk management, internal audit, enterprise performance, and the value of information. He is also a coach and mentor to individuals and organizations around the world.

Norman has been honored as a Fellow of the Open Compliance and Ethics Group and an Honorary Fellow of the Institute of Risk Management for his contributions to risk management.

He is the author of five earlier books, all of which are available on Amazon:

- *World-Class Internal Audit: Tales from my* Journey

- *Management's Guide to Sarbanes-Oxley Section 404: Maximize Value Within Your Organization* (described as "the best Sarbanes-Oxley 404 guide out there for management")

- *How Good is your GRC? Twelve Questions to Guide Executives, Boards, and Practitioners*, and

- *World-Class Risk Management*

- *Auditing that Matters*

Praise for *World-Class Risk Management* includes:

- Norman Marks' latest book "World-Class Risk Management" (2015) is a must read for anyone interested in this evolving topic. It will appeal to the beginner as it leads one from the basics through the various concepts and techniques, while it challenges the most serious practitioner to re-evaluate what they do and why. The academic will also benefit from using this book because of the exhaustive references to some of the best source material on this topic. Norman challenges many stereotypical and clichéd views on risk management, but keeps coming back to simple, easy to understand concepts. He captures the essence of his thinking in "The management of risk is an essential element in successful management." (page 13). This book makes you think, yet it is written in a lucid and friendly style. His thinking on 'risk appetite' challenges some 'sacred cows' held by many, but will help those who have struggled with this concept to find better ways of approaching this controversial subject. I wish he had written more on risk workshops but that may be another book someday. Well done, Norman, and thank you for sharing your experience, research and thinking.

- A very refreshing view of how risk management should be. Packed with a lot of good insights and force us to re-examine the way we think of risk management, its value to an organisation and to be relevant to the organisation objectives.

Norman's blog is at normanmarks.wordpress.com.

reputation, 17, 23, 35, 42, 43, 58
risk, 3, 4, 5, 6, 7, 10, 11, 12, 14, 15, 16,
18, 19, 20, 21, 23, 24, 25, 26, 27, 28,
32, 33, 34, 35, 36, 37, 38, 39, 40, 41,
42, 43, 44, 45, 46, 47, 48, 49, 50, 51,
52, 53, 54, 55, 56, 57, 58, 59, 60, 61,
63, 64, 66, 67
Risk, 1, 3, 5, 7, 10, 11, 15, 20, 25, 27, 28,
30, 34, 37, 44, 45, 46, 47, 48, 50, 53,
54, 55, 56, 57, 64
risk appetite, 11, 39, 40, 54, 55, 56, 59
risk hunter, 25

risk profile, 10, 56
risk register, 10

S

strategy, 6, 13, 46, 50, 56, 65
supply chain, 12, 22, 38

W

workshops, 31

CPSIA information can be obtained
at www.ICGtesting.com
Printed in the USA
LVHW070619020420
651997LV00005B/651